My Name is Sophia

A Collection of Stories about People who Share my Name

By Allison Dearstyne

Dedicated to every girl named Sophia; may you grow up to be wise.

The name Sophia comes from Ancient Greece and means "wisdom." The first known records come from the 4th century. Originally, the Greeks defined wisdom as having cleverness and skill. The great thinker Plato shaped the meaning of your name further when he used the word "philosophy" to describe the "love of wisdom." The Eastern Orthodox and Catholic Churches use the term "Hagia Sophia" or "Holy Wisdom" to describe God. Later, a variation of the name's spelling emerged, "Sofia." The capital city of Bulgaria is spelled this way!

In this book, we will look at these seven outstanding women who shaped history and share your name:

Sophia Duleep Singh
Sophia Jex-Blake
Sophia Danenberg
Sophia Hayden
Sofia Kovalevskaya
Sophia Laskaridou
Sophia Angeli Nelson

Sophia Duleep Singh was an Indian British princess and suffragette who rocked her world! She was born in London in 1876 to a diverse and privileged family. Her father was the last Maharaja, or ruler, of the Sikh Empire and had been forced to give his kingdom to the British when he was a child. Her father had moved to England, where he was treated kindly by Queen Victoria. When her father grew up, he married Sophia's mother, a woman with mixed African and European ancestry.

Little Sophia's childhood was unique. Her Indian, African and European cultures were mixed with a British noble upbringing. Queen Victoria always liked the Singh family, especially her little goddaughter Sophia. When Sophia was a child, her mother died, and her father tried to return with his family to India. But the British did not allow it, and when they caught the Singh family on their way to India, they were arrested for leaving. When Queen Victoria brought them back to England, she taught the Singh sisters to become proper British ladies. Wildly popular wherever they went, they attended parties in fancy dresses and enjoyed British forms of entertainment. As a young woman, Sophia Duleep Singh loved the carefree posh lifestyle of British royalty.

But things changed in 1903 when she secretly dodged the British and traveled to India with her sister. This trip was a turning point in her life; she met her relatives and was faced with the harsh realities of colonial rule in India. She saw how much her family and country had lost when her father surrendered to the British. She witnessed poverty and racism against the Indians by the British. After attending a party for Mahatma Gandhi, she was spurred on by him to demand equal rights. By the end of her trip, Sophia Duleep Singh had turned against the British Empire. When she returned to England, things were never the same.

Protesting the unfair laws, she refused to pay taxes to England. She became a suffragette, which is someone who fights for the right of women to vote. Sophia Duleep Singh acted first for women in England and then for women in the colonies of the British Empire around the world. Using her fame as a princess to help her cause, she sold a suffragette newspaper outside of the mansion in England where she was raised.

Officials in the British government became annoyed with her, and King George V was completely frustrated that he couldn't control her. She put the government officials in a tough predicament; they wanted to arrest her, but they wouldn't because of her popularity and special relationship to British royalty. Sophia Duleep Singh spent years bravely challenging laws that she knew to be unfair.

In 1928 her hard work paid off when the Equal Franchise Act was passed, allowing women over the age of 21 to vote. Sophia Duleep Singh described her major life goal as the advancement of women. She could have chosen to continue living a comfortable life as royalty, but instead she chose to work hard for a cause she found worthwhile. Sophia Duleep Singh played a significant role at an important time in India and England's long history.

When you are old enough to vote in elections, cast your ballot and think about brave Sophia Duleep Singh!

Sophia Jex-Blake was an English physician and feminist. Born in 1840 in Hastings to wealthy parents, she had the privilege of being educated by tutors. Like other girls, she was expected to marry young and work only in her home. But that was not the life Sophia Jex-Blake wanted! She begged her parents to allow her to attend college, but they wouldn't permit it.

Determined to pursue her dream, Sophia Jex-Blake traveled to the United States to learn what she could about medicine. She applied to Harvard University and was rejected because she was a woman. Then her father died, which led Sophia Jex-Blake to return to England. Still, she didn't forget her dream.

In Scotland, views on educating women were a little more progressive. So, she applied to the University of Edinburgh, and they accepted her application - at first. But upon finding out that she would be the only female student, they rejected her, saying they could not make arrangements for just one woman.

Sophia Jex-Blake didn't let that stop her! She arranged for a local newspaper to run an advertisement for other young women to apply to the school. As she had hoped, more women applied, and they studied medicine too. These brave women became known as the Edinburgh Seven.

Sophia Jex-Blake found that her struggle to study medicine was far from over. The Edinburgh Seven were harassed by mobs who hurled mud and trash at them in the streets. The women were followed home, where they found fireworks attached to their front doors. They had gates slammed in their faces by people who tried to prevent them from taking their exams. Some of the male students were shocked by how badly the women were treated and acted like their bodyguards, escorting them to and from class every day.

In 1873, after a lot of hard work and perseverance, the Edinburgh Seven completed their requirements for graduation. But the University refused to give them degrees on the basis that as women, they never should have been allowed to enter the school at all. This decision was reversed in 1874 and Sophia Jex-Blake began practicing medicine as Edinburgh's first woman doctor.

She established a clinic that became known as the Edinburgh Hospital and Dispensary for Women. This clinic opened its doors to all women, including the poor. Sophia Jex-Blake was determined to make medical care affordable by charging only a small fee, compared to the other expensive local hospitals and clinics. The hospital was the first to be run entirely for women, entirely by women. Sophia Jex-Blake found joy in her work helping others.

Today there are many women doctors! We learn from Sophia Jex-Blake to persist. When the going gets tough, find a way to keep going and you can be like strong Sophia Jex-Blake!

Sophia Danenberg is an American mountain climber who has the distinction of being the first Black person to summit Mount Everest! She was born Sophia Scott in Illinois in 1972 to a Japanese mother and Black American father. Long before she got into hiking, she was a great student and studied environmental sciences and public policy at Harvard University and then Keio University in Japan.

She moved back to the United States and began a successful career improving clean energy. Sophia Danenberg's friend encouraged her to try rock climbing as a hobby, and she loved it! She began climbing at her local Appalachian Mountain Club Chapter where she met her husband, David Danenberg. They summited some of the world's most famous mountains together, and then she decided to tackle the biggest mountain in the world: Mount Everest. Located in Nepal, Mount Everest stands 29,000 feet high. Sophia Danenberg was in her mid-thirties and only trained for a few weeks to prepare for the treacherous climb.

She faced some challenges in her training! She worked full-time while preparing and purchasing equipment. She couldn't find a down suit small enough to fit her, so she hiked in one that was way too big. Unlike most people who climb Everest, she did the hike unguided and made a lot of tough decisions on her own. On May 19, 2006, suffering from bronchitis, frostbite on her cheeks, and a clogged oxygen mask, Sophia Danenberg reached the top of Mount Everest.

Amazingly, Sophia Danenberg didn't know at the time of her hike that she was the first Black person to summit Mount Everest! She didn't do it to chase fame; she simply loved to climb. In an interview after the hike, she noted the lack of diversity in the climbing community. She hopes to help change that!

Wherever you live, you can try taking hikes through the woods, mountains, or try a rock-climbing wall at local gym. Then you can be like the little lady who climbed the world's biggest mountain, Sophia Danenberg!

Sophia Hayden was a talented Latin American architect. Born in Chile in 1868 to a Chilean mother and American father, she was sent to live with her grandparents in Boston when she was six. In high school, she was interested in building design and later became the first woman to graduate with a degree in architecture at the Massachusetts Institute of Technology.

When she tried to get a job, she faced discrimination because no one wanted to hire a woman architect. Rather than finding low-paying entry level work, Sophia Hayden became a mechanical drawing teacher at a high school. This wasn't what she really wanted to do with her talent. But when she was 21, she got a chance to shine!

A competition opened for contestants to enter designs for the Woman's Building at the World's Columbian Exposition in Chicago. At the time, it was the only real design competition that women were allowed to enter. Basing her design on a project from college, "Renaissance Museum of Fine Arts," Sophia Hayden designed a two-story building with pavilions, arches, columned terraces and some other classical features. The building was truly beautiful! She won first prize out of 13 entries submitted by women and earned $1,000 for her design. Men who designed similar buildings won $10,000 for their work, which shows how hard things were for career women back in those days.

After the project was completed, Sophia Hayden got mixed reviews. On one hand, she was praised by some for her artistic taste, delicacy of style, and elegant interior. On the other hand, she was criticized for making the building look "too feminine." To them, the elegant structure of the building was proof women were not fit to be architects. Sadly, her structure was torn down along with other buildings from the fair after only a year. Later Sophia Hayden married and adopted her husband's daughter. She lived a quiet, happy life as an artist back in Massachusetts.

Sophia Hayden didn't get to fully reap the rewards of being a successful architect, but she broke ground in a career that had previously been reserved only for men. When you see a building that is beautifully designed, think about its architect and think about Sophia Hayden!

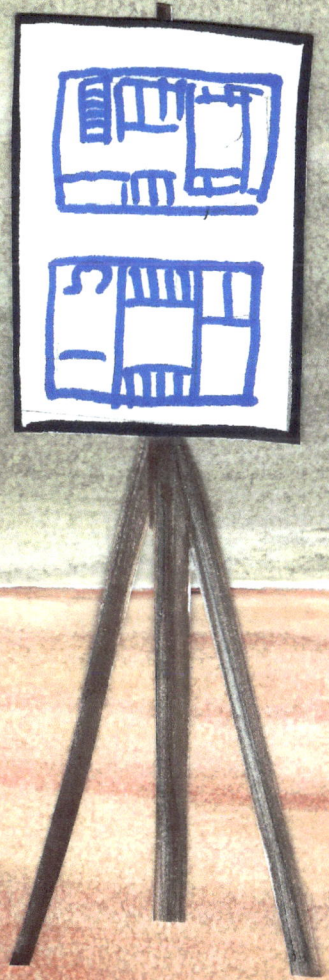

Sofia Kovalevskaya was a Russian mathematician known as greatest woman scientist before the twentieth century. She was born Sofia Vasilyevna in Moscow in 1850 to a wealthy family. Her parents valued education, and from the beginning, she was a math whiz. Little Sofia loved to read her father's physics and math notes from his college days. She learned English, French and German from her governesses, and she learned math from a private tutor.

Sofia Kovalevskaya impressed all her tutors with her amazing ability to figure out complex equations. Despite her obvious talent, in Russia women were not allowed to attend universities or study abroad without permission from their husbands. She solved this problem by marrying Vladmir Kovalevsky, a paleontologist who helped her move to Germany to further her studies.

There, she studied under great professors privately and presented three papers to get her doctorate degree. The papers covered a broad range of topics, from calculus to mechanics to way Saturn's rings are evolving. Sofia Kovalevskaya graduated at the top of her class! Especially noteworthy was her paper on partial differential equations, which made huge contributions to mathematics and is now called Cauchy-Kovalevskaya theorem. In contrast to what most people think about mathematics, Sofia Kovalevskaya saw the subject as a form of poetry and art.

She said, "Many who have had an opportunity of knowing any more about mathematics confuse it with arithmetic, and consider it an arid science. In reality, however, it is a science which requires a great amount of imagination."

Later, she became a professor at Stockholm University - the first woman to hold such a position. She wrote books on mathematics, plays and a memoir. A vibrant feminist, she fought for women's rights and made great progress!

When you are in your math classes at school, pay close attention and you can excel like smart Sofia Kovalevskaya!

Sophia Laskaridou was a Greek artist known for her talent in painting impressionistic landscapes of countrysides. She was born in Athens in 1876 into a wealthy and cultured family. Believing in equal education for girls, Sophia's mother founded a girls' school that introduced physical education into the curriculum. It was the first school in Athens to have a well-rounded education for girls!

As a little girl, Sophia Laskaridou loved art. As she grew, she especially loved painting landscapes of the beautiful country where she lived. She entered her work into exhibitions where her talent was recognized, and then she decided to study art abroad.

Delighted to receive a scholarship for her work, she traveled to Germany and France to study under great teachers. There, Sophia Laskaridou was influenced by great artists like Pablo Picasso and Auguste Renoir. Her painting style shows the influence of impressionism, which is painting with small, thin brush strokes in such a way to emphasize light. She still loved to paint landscapes, but she expanded her subjects to include portraits, still lifes, and genre scenes, which portray beauty in everyday life.

When she returned to Greece in 1916, she had great success selling her paintings. Most artists, even great ones, are not fully appreciated during their lifetime. Not so for Sophia Laskaridou, who became a national celebrity! Try finding a scenic spot outside to paint a landscape, and you can be like artistic Sophia Laskaridou!

Sophia Angeli Nelson is a Black American author, journalist, lawyer, and political strategist. She was born in 1967 in Germany. A military kid, she moved several times in her childhood before attending San Diego State University in California. There, she became the first Black woman elected to a major position in student government. After graduating with a bachelor's degree in political history, she attended law school at American University Washington College of Law.

She became a lawyer in New Jersey and went on to win the Republican nomination for Congress but had to withdraw because of illness. She enjoyed a career as a lawyer for nine years, and then decided to become a journalist and author. She became the first White House journalist for *Jet* magazine and wrote columns for several newspapers.

History was made in 2008 when Illinois Senator Barack Obama was elected President, and Sophia Angeli Nelson had the honor of reporting on his campaign! She continued to climb in her career, serving as senior committee staff counsel in the House of Representatives. Later she was a director of congressional and public affairs for the Chamber of Commerce.

She enjoyed these positions, and then in 2011, she wrote her first book, *Black Woman Redefined: Dispelling Myths and Discovering Fulfillment in the Age of Michelle Obama*. Sophia Angeli Nelson recognizes the lack of Black women in many important roles in society, and her goal is to help change that. Today, Sophia Angeli Nelson is a highly sought-after speaker and political commentator on major news networks. A lot of people value her informed opinion!

Develop the good habit of writing often and you can be like successful Sophia Angeli Nelson!

This page is all about you!

_____ was born on

_____

As a baby, Sophia _____

_____

As a little girl, Sophia _____

_____

Sophia is especially good at _____

_____

Sophia is often described as _____

_____

Sophia makes people laugh when she _____

_____

One day Sophia would like to _____

_____

This page is for making a self-portrait. A self-portrait is a picture of you, drawn by you!

Bibliography

Anand, Anita. "Sophia Duleep Singh: princess and suffragette." *bl.uk* British Library. 06 Feb. 2018. Web. 03 Feb. 2019.

Brenton, Felix. "Danenberg, Sophia (1972-). *BlackPast.org.* BlackPast Remembered & Reclaimed. Web. 29 Dec. 2018.

Enclyclopaedia Britannica Editors. "Sophia Hayden." *Enclyclopaedia Britannica.* Enclyclopaedia Britannica, inc. 30 Jan. 2019. Web. 01 Feb. 2019.

Enclyclopaedia Britannica Editors. "Sofya Vasilyevna Kovalevskaya." *Enclyclopaedia Britannica.* Enclyclopaedia Britannica, inc. 11 Jan. 2019. Web. 01 Feb. 2019.

McCullins, Darren. "Sophia Jex-Blake: The battle to be Scotland's first female doctor" *BBC Scotland.* 6 Nov. 2018. Web. 29 Dec. 2018.

Mitchell, Adam. "Conversation with Sophia Danenberg: First African American to Climb Everest." *Melanin Base Camp.* 31 Jan. 2018. Web. 29 Dec. 2018.

Momodu, Samuel. "Sophia Angeli Nelson (1967-). *BlackPast.org.* BlackPast Remembered & Reclaimed,

Wikipedia contributors. "Sophia (given name)." *Wikipedia, The Free Encyclopedia.* Wikipedia, The Free Encyclopedia, 19 Dec. 2018. Web. 29 Dec. 2018.

Wikipedia contributors. "Sophia (wisdom)." *Wikipedia, The Free Encyclopedia*. Wikipedia, The Free Encyclopedia, 13 Dec. 2018. Web. 29 Dec. 2018.

Wikipedia contributors. "Sophia Danenberg." *Wikipedia, The Free Encyclopedia*. Wikipedia, The Free Encyclopedia, 22 Dec. 2017. Web. 29 Dec. 2018.

Wikipedia contributors. "Sophia Hayden." *Wikipedia, The Free Encyclopedia*. Wikipedia, The Free Encyclopedia, 7 Dec. 2018. Web. 01 Feb. 2019.

Wikipedia contributors. "Sophia Jex-Blake." *Wikipedia, The Free Encyclopedia*. Wikipedia, The Free Encyclopedia, 10 Dec. 2018. Web. 02 Jan. 2019.

Wikipedia contributors. "Sofia Kovalevskaya." *Wikipedia, The Free Encyclopedia*. Wikipedia, The Free Encyclopedia, 15 Jan. 2019. Web. 01 Feb. 2019.

Wikipedia contributors. "Sophia Laskaridou." *Wikipedia, The Free Encyclopedia*. Wikipedia, The Free Encyclopedia, 12 Jun. 2018. Web. 06 Feb. 2019.

Wikipedia contributors. "Sophia A. Nelson." *Wikipedia, The Free Encyclopedia*. Wikipedia, The Free Encyclopedia, 29 Jan. 2019. Web. 04 Feb. 2019.

Wikipedia contributors. "Sophia Duleep Singh." *Wikipedia, The Free Encyclopedia*. Wikipedia, The Free Encyclopedia, 19 Jan. 2019. Web. 04 Feb. 2019.

www.ingramcontent.com/pod-product-compliance
Lightning Source LLC
Chambersburg PA
CBHW042111040426

42448CB00002B/229